Cool SHELLS

Creating Fun *and* Fascinating Collections!

Mary Elizabeth Salzmann

ABDO
Publishing Company

Published by ABDO Publishing Company, 4940 Viking Drive, Edina, Minnesota 55435.
Copyright © 2007 by Abdo Consulting Group, Inc. International copyrights reserved in all countries.
No part of this book may be reproduced in any form without written permission from the publisher.
The Checkerboard Library™ is a trademark and logo of ABDO Publishing Company.

Printed in the United States.

Design and Production: Mighty Media, Inc.
Cover Photos: Anders Hanson
Interior Photos: Anders Hanson; Shutterstock; Mollusk image (p. 4) © Franco Banfi / SeaPics.com; The following manufacturers/names appearing in Cool Shells are trademarks: Dawn® (p. 21), Johnson's® Baby Oil (p.21)
Series Editor: Pam Price

Library of Congress Cataloging-in-Publication Data

Salzmann, Mary Elizabeth, 1968-
  Cool shells / Mary Elizabeth Salzmann.
      p. cm. -- (Cool collections)
  Includes index.
  ISBN-13: 978-1-59679-772-7
  ISBN-10: 1-59679-772-X
 1. Shells--Juvenile literature. 2. Shells--Collection and preservation--Juvenile literature. I. Title. II. Series: Cool collections (Edina, Minn.)

    QL405.2.S25 2007
    594.147'7--dc22   2006011966

Contents

What Is a Seashell?

A SEASHELL IS THE HARD OUTER CASE OF A SEA CREATURE CALLED A MOLLUSK. There are many different kinds of mollusks. What they all have in common is that they don't have skeletons or bones. Instead, they grow shells that protect their soft bodies. They have special muscles that attach their bodies to their shells. Snails, clams, and oysters are a few examples of mollusks.

Fast Facts

- There are more than 150,000 species of mollusks.
- Mollusks have existed for 600 million years.

Seashells in History

PEOPLE HAVE BEEN FASCINATED BY SHELLS FOR THOUSANDS OF YEARS. Shells have been used for various purposes on nearly every continent. Cowrie shells were used as money as early as 2000 BC, during the Chinese **Bronze Age**. Shells were still used as money in parts of Africa until almost AD 1900. Shells were also used for ceremonies and **rituals**, art, and decoration.

Cowrie shells

Written Relic

The Chinese character for the word *shell* also appears in the character for *money*.

贝 财

"shell"   "money"

Why Collect Seashells?

COLLECTING SEASHELLS IS A VERY POPULAR HOBBY.
Some people just like the way the shells look. Some people enjoy picking them up when they go to the beach. Others like to study the differences between shells and learn about the animals that made them.

Some collectors specialize in certain types of shells. Other collectors try to collect as many different types of shells as possible. There is no right or wrong reason to start a shell collection.

Shell collecting is generally an inexpensive hobby. If you live near a beach, it may not cost you anything to collect shells.

Nutmeg shell

Cone shell

Top shell

Deciding What to Collect

It's up to you to decide what kind of shell collection you want to have. You may want to collect certain species of shells or maybe shells from certain locations. Or, you can collect all kinds of shells.

The types of seashells you collect may depend on where you live or go on vacation. Beaches in California have different shells from beaches in Texas, Florida, and New Jersey. Still other shells are available on beaches in countries outside the United States, such as Mexico, France, and Greece.

However, it is not even necessary to go to a beach to collect shells. There are stores and Web sites that sell shells. Or maybe you have a friend or relative who lives near a beach and can send shells to you. Once you've started your collection, you can trade shells with other collectors.

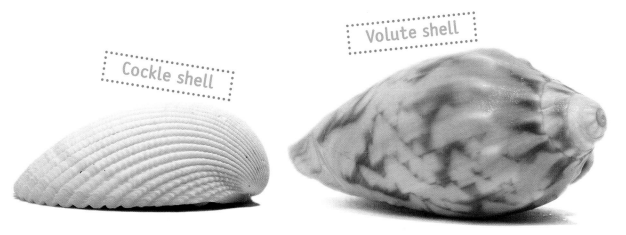

Cockle shell

Volute shell

Collecting Responsibly

Auger shells

IT IS IMPORTANT TO COLLECT SEASHELLS RESPONSIBLY. Responsible shell collectors care about the environment. They help preserve mollusk species and their **habitats**.

Take It or Leave It?

There are some beaches where you're not allowed to remove shells. Other beaches may let you take only certain types of shells. Or, they may limit the number of shells you can take. So make sure you find out the rules for the beaches where you look for shells.

Once you learn that it's okay to take shells from a beach, take only a few examples of each type of shell you want to collect. Don't try to take home every shell on the beach!

A Photo Is Forever

If you are going to a beach where you can't keep the shells, take a camera to photograph the shells you find. You can also make sketches of the shells. Take a notebook and pencils, markers, or crayons.

Be a Choosy Buyer

LIVING MOLLUSKS

Most shells you find on the beach are empty. The mollusks that lived in them have died, and only the shells are left. However, sometimes you

When you buy shells, try to make sure that the seller got the shells responsibly. Trade shells only with other responsible collectors.

might find a shell that still has the mollusk living in it. This happens most often when you look for shells in tide pools or in the wet sand along the water's edge.

It's best to study live mollusks in their natural **habitat**. Don't take them from the beach. You can photograph or sketch them and include the pictures in your collection.

Leave Things the Way You Find Them

As you look for shells, try not to disturb the beach more than necessary. If you turn over a piece of coral or a rock to look underneath it, make sure you put it back the way you found it. Living creatures may need it for shade or protection. Also, some sea animals lay their eggs on the underside of rocks and coral. The eggs will not survive if left exposed to sun and predators.

Finally, make sure you don't leave any trash on the beach. Take along a trash bag. You could even pick up any litter you find while you are looking for shells.

Growing Your Collection

SHELL COLLECTING, LIKE ANY OTHER COLLECTING HOBBY, IS AN ONGOING PROCESS. You can keep adding to your collection for years. You may add shells frequently and spend a lot of time organizing and updating your collection. Or maybe you get new shells only once a year when you're on vacation. It's up to you how much time you spend working with your collection.

As you learn about different shells, you may decide to add new categories of shells to your collection. Perhaps you've lost interest in some types of shells. You might be able to trade those to another collector. In exchange, ask for examples of the new shells you want to collect.

Over time your collection will grow. Finding enough space for it may become a problem! You might have to get rid of some shells to make room for new ones. Another option is to display only some of your shells. Keep the rest of your collection packed away.

Research and Resources

YOU MAY DECIDE TO COLLECT SHELLS JUST BECAUSE THEY LOOK COOL. Or you may think it's fun to find them on the beach. Those are **valid** reasons to start a shell collection. However, if you want to go further and learn more about shells, there are many resources available to you.

Books

You can find many books about seashells and shell collecting at a bookstore or a library.

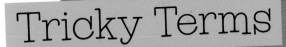

Worm shell

FIELD GUIDES

A shell field guide can help you identify exactly what species of shells you have. Each field guide will be a little different. But, they all should include a picture of each shell, the scientific name for the species, where it can be found, and a brief description of the shell. If you know you will be going to a certain area, you can use a field guide to see what shell species you're likely to find there.

Tricky Terms

The study of mollusks is called malacology.

The study and collection of shells is called conchology.

11

OTHER BOOKS

A field guide is an important resource because you'll be able to identify most shells you find. However, it won't provide much information beyond physical descriptions of the shells. There are many other aspects of mollusks, seashells, and shell collecting that you can learn about through books. For example, you can find out what mollusks eat. And you can read about why their shells are shaped the way they are. There are also books that have ideas for organizing and storing your collection.

THE INTERNET

There are many Web sites devoted to mollusks, seashells, and shell collecting. Some are maintained by individual collectors. Others may belong to a club, organization, aquarium, zoo, or museum. There are also online shell field guides.

Ask an Adult

Ask a parent, guardian, or teacher for permission before you send an e-mail or any information about yourself to a Web site.

Keep in mind who wrote the information you're reading. A Web site run by a **reputable** organization is more likely to be correct than an individual's site. It's a good idea to confirm facts by finding them on more than one site.

However, collectors' Web sites may have interesting stories about their shells and collecting experiences. The sites may have good ideas for organizing shells or fun things to do with shells. So, depending on the kind of information you want, both types of Web sites are good resources.

Clubs and shows

There are clubs for shell collectors throughout the United States and in other countries. Joining a club lets you meet other shell collectors. You can discuss shell collecting and trade shells. Some clubs have activities such as shell exhibits, beach cleanups, and field trips. A shell-collecting club may also publish a magazine or a newsletter.

Shell events and exhibits are held every year in various states and countries. The shows are often sponsored or hosted by a shell club. At a shell show, you can see shell exhibits created by different collectors and dealers. You can meet other collectors and listen to experts talk about shells and collecting. You may even be able to exhibit, sell, or trade your own shells.

You can find out about shell clubs and events online or at the library.

Whelk shell

Finding Seashells

ONE OF THE THINGS SHELL COLLECTORS LIKE BEST IS SEARCHING FOR SEASHELLS. They love to walk on the beach looking for the perfect seashells for their collections. It's like a treasure hunt!

Tools for Collecting

The most important item to have when collecting shells is something to carry the shells in. Take along a bucket or pail. Here are some other useful tools.

SHOVEL OR RAKE
You can use a shovel or a rake to dig in the sand for buried shells and mollusks.

CAMERA
If you can't remove the shells from the beach, you can take pictures of the shells and mollusks you find. You can also photograph the locations where you find shells that you do keep.

NET
A net can be handy for picking up shells in tide pools.

NOTEBOOK
Many collectors like to make notes about where they found each of their shells. You can include sketches and descriptions of the shells you find. You could also keep a journal of your collecting experiences.

Where to Look

The best place to look for seashells is along the shoreline. Good times to look for seashells are during low tide and right after a storm. You can find shells trapped in shallow pools around rocks or coral.

Another area to find shells is along the high-tide mark on the beach. Look for an uneven line of seaweed, shells, driftwood, and other **debris** from the ocean. The waves push them up onto the beach. They get left behind when the tide goes down.

Beachcombing Rules

1. Make sure you are allowed to be on the beach. Don't go onto private beaches unless you have permission from the owner.

2. Find out if there are any restrictions on shell removal. If the beach is in a state or national park, ask a park ranger. If the beach is in a town, call the police station or city hall to ask about shelling restrictions. Shops that sell or rent diving and fishing gear are also good places to ask for information.

3. There may also be signs posted on the beach telling you what you can and cannot do. Always follow the rules for any beach you visit.

4. If you are going to wade near rocks or coral, wear shoes to protect your feet.

5. For safety, do not go to the beach alone. Never go into the water unless an adult is present.

Buying Seashells

Scallop shells

IF YOU WANT TO COLLECT SEASHELLS BUT CAN'T GO TO A BEACH, YOU CAN BUY SHELLS. Or you can buy shells to **supplement** the shells you do find. Purchasing shells doesn't have to be very expensive. Although rare seashells can cost hundreds of dollars, most shells are only a few dollars each.

Scientific Names

Many shell collectors and sellers use the scientific names for the different families and species of seashells. For example, the scientific family name for scallop shells is Pectinidae. Within this family, there are many species. So, if you want to collect different kinds of scallops, you will need to know the names of the species you want to add to your collection.

Some examples of Pectinidae species are *Pecten diegensis*, *Pecten ziczac*, and *Pecten raveneli*. You can use a field guide to learn the scientific names of seashells.

Seashell Value

It is important to learn how to tell what a shell is worth. Then you will know you're paying a fair price for shells you buy. And you'll be able to ask a fair price or exchange for shells you sell or trade.

It's a good idea to make a list of the shells you'd like to buy and how much each one is likely to cost. Keep your list with you when you are shell shopping. It will help you to remember what shells you want for your collection. It could also keep you from impulsively buying a shell you don't really want or need.

Online Seashell Catalogs

There are a number of Web sites that offer online catalogs of seashells. If your parent or guardian says it's okay, you can order shells from these sites. Even if you can't buy the shells online, these catalogs make it easy to find the value of shells you have or want to buy.

Seashell Grading

Two main factors determine the value of a shell. Those are its rarity and its condition. Say you have two examples of the same species of shell, and one of them is faded or broken and the other isn't. The faded, broken one will be worth less than the undamaged one.

Most shells offered for sale or trade by shell collectors and dealers are graded. This means that each shell is given a rating based on its condition. The most common shell grading system used is called HMS-ISGS. This system has four levels of quality.

Gem (G): The shell was collected when the mollusk was alive. The mollusk was an adult when it was collected. The shell is of the typical size and color of its species. The shell doesn't have any visible flaws or chips. The shell has been well cleaned.

Fine (F): The criteria are the same as for a gem-quality shell, except that it may have a few minor flaws. The flaws cannot have been repaired or altered in any way.

Good (Gd): The same criteria as for a fine-quality shell, but it may have more flaws. Also, it may have been collected when the mollusk was not fully adult. Otherwise the shell must be typical of its species.

Commercial (C): Shells collected after the mollusk died are rated commercial. The shell may be chipped, faded, or otherwise imperfect. It is not considered a collector's specimen. It cannot be sold through a mail-order catalog.

Collectors use plus signs to indicate that a shell falls between two of the grades. For example, a shell marked F+ is better than fine quality but not quite gem quality.

Seashell Shows and Conventions

Shows sponsored by seashell clubs are good places to buy shells. There are usually many collectors and **vendors** showing and selling their shells. Make sure you bring the list of shells you want to add to your collection. Not only can you buy shells at a shell show but you can also ask questions. It's a great way to learn more about mollusks, shells, and collecting.

You can search online for locations and dates of shell shows. The newspaper may list them in an events calendar. And, you may be able to find information about shell events at the library.

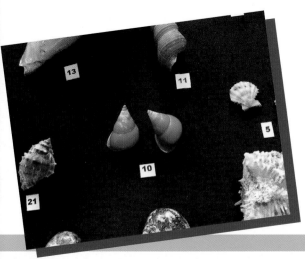

Retail Stores

Unless you're in a town near the ocean, it may be hard to find a store that sells seashells. Look in the telephone book for stores. Check categories such as hobbies, **collectibles**, crafts, and souvenirs. A librarian may also be able to help you find local shell retailers.

Trading and Selling Seashells

A FUN ASPECT TO ANY KIND OF COLLECTING IS TRADING WITH OTHER COLLECTORS. Maybe some of your friends collect shells. Or you can meet other shell collectors by joining a shell club or attending a shell show. If you're going to be seeing other collectors, bring along any shells that you're willing to trade. Don't forget the list of seashells you want to add to your collection.

You can also sell the shells you don't want anymore. Then you can use the money from the sales to buy other shells.

Online Trading and Selling

There are some seashell Web sites that let collectors list their own shells for sale or trade. You could also try selling your shells on a shopping Web site such as eBay. Always ask a parent or other adult for permission before you post any information about yourself or your collection on any Web site.

Cleaning Seashells

ANY SHELLS YOU FIND ON THE BEACH HAVE TO BE THOROUGHLY CLEANED. Otherwise, they may start to stink!

1. Rinse your shells thoroughly with a hose or a faucet. Use the force of the water to push out anything that is stuck inside the shells.

2. Soak the shells in a solution of half water and half bleach for about 24 hours. Then rinse the shells again. You should get help from an adult when using bleach. Bleach can be harmful if you breathe it in or get it on your skin.

3. Use dish soap, warm water, and an old, soft toothbrush to clean the outsides of the shells.

4. After the shells have dried completely, you can rub them with mineral oil to bring out the shine. Baby oil is one kind of mineral oil.

Storage and Organization

A SEASHELL'S COLOR WILL FADE OVER TIME IF IT IS EXPOSED TO STRONG LIGHT, ESPECIALLY SUNLIGHT. It's best to keep your shells in boxes or drawers. Line the boxes or drawers with cotton or tissue to cushion the shells and keep them from sliding around too much. It's not good for shells to get too dusty. Keeping them covered will help limit the amount of dust that gets on them.

Seashell Storage Ideas

- Use smaller boxes to divide a larger box or a drawer into sections for your shells. Matchboxes or jewelry gift boxes work well as dividers.

- You can buy cabinets with small drawers or compartments for sorting and organizing things. Look for them at craft stores and hardware stores. There are also stores that specialize in products for organization and storage.

Personalize It!

Use paint, markers, stickers, and other craft items to decorate your seashell storage boxes.

22

Organizing and Labeling

You should have a system for organizing your collection. Most collectors keep shells of the same family and species together. For example, you could put olive shells in one box or drawer and cockle shells in another.

Each of your shells should be labeled so it's easy to keep track of what shells you have. At the very least, you should label each shell with its name. But there is a lot of other information you could include to make your records more complete and interesting.

LABEL INFORMATION

- The scientific family and species names for the shell

- Where the shell was found

- The date the shell was found

- If you acquired the shell from someone else, the name of the person you got it from and whether is was a gift or you bought it or traded for it

- The date you acquired the shell

- The value of the shell

- Anything else you want to remember about the shell

Computerize It!

There may not be enough room to put a label with all this information with each shell. In that case, give each of your shells a number. Then record the number and the information about each shell in a notebook. If you need to know about a certain shell in your collection, you can look it up by its number.

You can also record information about your shells in a computer **database** program. When information is in a database, you can sort it different ways. For example, you can find all the shells of a certain species or all the shells found in the same location. A parent or other adult may be able to help you set up a computer database for your shell collection.

Displaying Seashells

TOO MUCH LIGHT AND DUST ISN'T GOOD FOR SEASHELLS. So, you have to be careful about how you display your collection. You may decide to keep the shells in their boxes or drawers all the time. Then you just get them out when you want to show them to others or look at them yourself. But there are ways to display your shells while limiting any possible damage.

First, find a place to display your shells that doesn't get direct sunlight. A corner away from windows is a good choice. A bookcase or a cabinet with glass doors provides extra protection from light and dust. Once you've picked the location, there are two basic methods for displaying your seashells. You can choose one method or a combination of both methods.

Displaying Duplicate Seashells

If you have two examples of a seashell species, you could keep one example in its box and display the other. This method works best for collectors who have a lot of the same types of shells. The advantage is that you can leave the shells out all the time. And you know that your best examples of each shell are stored safely away from light and dust.

Seashell Rotation

If you don't have a lot of **duplicate** shells in your collection, you can display just a few shells at a time. Put some of your shells in the display area for a few days or a week. Then put them away and replace them with different shells. This way you can show off your collection without constantly exposing your shells to light and dust. It's a good idea to gently wipe any dust off the shells with a soft cloth before putting them away.

Seashell Crafts

YOU CAN MAKE A LOT OF FUN
THINGS USING SEASHELLS.
Here are a few suggestions.

Seashell Jewelry

STEPS

1. Cut a piece of cord the length you want your jewelry to be.

2. String the shells on the cord. If necessary, you can have an adult help you punch a hole in a shell using a sharp tool such as an awl. If you are using a cowrie shell, poke the cord into the opening in the back with a toothpick. Fill the shell with craft glue to hold the cord in place. Wait for the glue to dry.

3. Add beads to make your jewelry unique.

4. Tie the ends of the cord together or attach a clasp. Craft stores sell many kinds of clasps for making jewelry.

What You Need

- One or more seashells
- Cord or string
- Beads
- Clasps or other **findings**

Seashell Critters

STEPS

1. Select shells that can be used to make a critter. Look for shells that could be the body, legs, and ears. You may have to try several different combinations.

2. You can use small bits of clay to temporarily hold the shells together to see how it looks.

3. After you have found the right combination of shells to make your critter, glue the parts together. Apply the glue to the shells with the tip of a toothpick. This makes it easier to put the glue exactly where you want it.

4. Make features by gluing on beads or craft eyes. Thread or thin wire could be whiskers. You could also use paints or markers to draw details on your critter.

5. If your critter doesn't stand up very well, glue its feet to a flat shell for a base.

What You Need

- A variety of seashells
- Decorations such as beads, plastic craft eyes, thread, and wire
- Polymer clay
- Craft glue
- Small paintbrush
- Markers or paints

Seashell Frames

STEPS

1. Remove the glass from the frame.

2. If you are using an unpainted wooden frame, you will need to paint it. Let the paint dry completely before going to step four.

3. Select seashells to decorate your frame. You can use a lot of shells or just a few.

4. Glue the seashells to the frame. For small shells, use the tip of a toothpick to put the glue on the shell.

What You Need

- Plain picture frame
- Seashells
- Craft glue
- Paint
- Clean, fine sand
- Paintbrushes

SAND BACKGROUND

1. Mix glue and sand together in an empty plastic container. Use about twice as much sand as glue.

2. With a brush, apply a layer of the mixture to the frame.

3. While it's still wet, push the shells into the sand layer. Then let the frame dry.

Craft or Collectible?

If you want to try some seashell crafts, make sure you use shells that you don't want to keep in your collection. Once you have used a shell in a craft project, it will no longer be a **collectible** shell.

Craft stores sell shells that are meant to be used in craft projects. This is a good way to make things with seashells without using shells from your collection.

Conclusion

THERE ARE AS MANY REASONS TO COLLECT SEASHELLS AS THERE ARE PEOPLE WHO COLLECT THEM. Some people like the way they look and use them for decoration. Some people like beachcombing and bringing home seashells they find. Some people enjoy the challenge of buying and trading with other collectors. Some people are interested in learning about the biology and the science of mollusks.

You may have other reasons for becoming a seashell collector. Once you start, though, you'll find it's a fascinating hobby that you can enjoy for a lifetime.

Glossary

Bronze Age – the period of time between the Stone Age and the Iron Age characterized by the use of bronze.

collectible – something that is valued or sought after by collectors.

database – a large collection of information.

debris – the remains of something after it has been destroyed.

duplicate – the same as another.

finding – a metal component used to make jewelry.

habitat – a place where a living thing is naturally found.

reputable – thought by others to have a good character.

ritual – a form or order to a ceremony.

supplement – something that improves or completes something else.

vendor – someone who sells things.

Web Sites

To learn more about collecting shells, visit ABDO Publishing on the World Wide Web at **www.abdopublishing.com**. Web sites about shell collecting are featured on our Book Links page. These links are routinely monitored and updated to provide the most current information available.

Index